CONTENTS

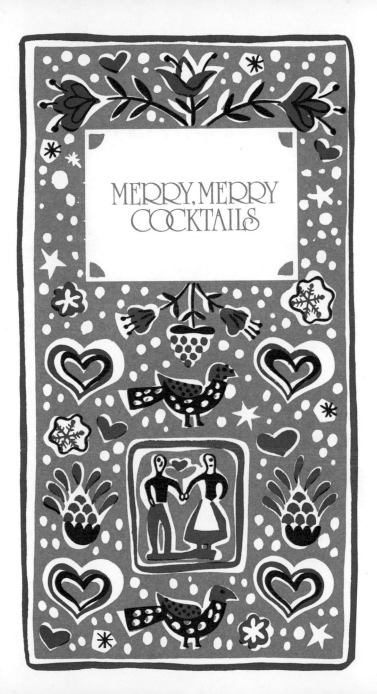

MERRY, MERRY COCKTAILS

COCKTAIL HINTS

Cocktails consist of a liquor — usually gin, whiskey or rum — with flavoring added. When the flavoring is lemon or lime juice, some sugar or sugar syrup is needed also.

Cocktails are usually served as appetizers or aperitifs, before a meal. Such cocktails should therefore be tart or "dry" to stimulate appetite. Such cocktails, being mostly liquor and only a small part flavoring or sweetening, are more potent as well as less sweet.

The following recipes are for strong, dry, cocktails. But there *are* times when sweeter, weaker cocktails are suitable. When your guests are not regular drinkers there should be more emphasis on fruit juices and sweetening than on liquor.

Any cocktail recipe can be modified to suit your taste and that of your guests. Sophisticated drinkers, as suggested above, like a lot of liquor and only a touch of flavoring; unsophisticated drinkers the other way around.

Most cocktails are at their best ice-cold: they should be shaken or stirred vigorously with ice-cubes (cracked or shaved ice is even better) and served promptly in thin, clean, stemmed glasses. Chilled glasses are an added refinement.

Cocktails like Martinis and Manhattans which contain only liquors, may be stirred vigorously with a rod or long spoon. Cocktails which contain fruit juices or eggs should be shaken in a shaker.

6

Use good fresh ice. Water exposed to odors while freezing will retain some of them and such ice-cubes will affect the drinks.

Put your ice in the shaker first; then pour the other ingredients over the ice.

Use good ingredients. The cost per drink is not much greater with the best of liquor.

Cocktails should not be made in advance if you can help yourself. If all your ingredients are lined up beforehand, the actual making is a very quick — and pleasantly social — process. The one ingredient which suffers by standing in readiness is fresh lemon or lime juice, which gets cloudy as it stands.

If you must make drinks in advance, do *not* add ice in advance, but shake or stir with ice when ready to serve.

It is better to make two or three small fresh shakers of cocktails than to make one large quantity and let it stand between drinks.

SWEETENING

Dry sugar does not dissolve easily in alcohol. Therefore in mixing sweetened drinks put in the sugar and non-alcoholic contents first, so the sugar can dissolve. If necessary, add a splash of water or soda to the sugar. A better and surer way to sweeten drinks is to prepare some Sugar Syrup beforehand—equal amounts of sugar and water, stirred, and left to dissolve. A spoon of syrup equals a spoon of sugar in any recipe.

Grenadine adds pinkness as well as sweetness, and must be used in moderation. The same is true of sweet flavorings like Falernum or Orgeat.

ON QUANTITIES

The normal drink of hard liquor is 1½ ounces and the normal cocktail glass 2 to 3½ ounces. The following recipes, on the strong side, usually specify 3 parts liquor to 1 part flavoring. Thus 1½ ounces liquor, plus ½ ounce flavoring, plus some melted ice and a spoon of sugar syrup, will nicely fill a small cocktail glass. If you use larger glasses, or want milder drinks, vary your quantities accórdingly. Please note that Martinis and Old-Fashioneds require more hard liquor than 1½ ounces for the normal serving.

Now Dasher, now Dancer!
Now, Prancer, and Vixen!
St. Nick's at the bar,
And the cocktails he's mixin'!

ABSINTHE COCKTAIL

3 parts Absinthe (Pernod)
2 parts Water
1 part Sugar Syrup

Shake with ice. Twist lemon peel over drink.

AQUAVIT MARTINI

5 parts Aquavit
1 part French (dry) Vermouth

Shake with ice. Twist lemon peel over drink.

ALEXANDER

1 part Gin
1 part Creme de Cacao
1 part Sweet Cream

Shake with ice. Brandy can be substituted for the gin.

APPLEJACK RABBIT

1 oz. Apple Brandy (or Applejack)
1/3 oz. Lemon Juice
1/3 oz. Orange Juice
Maple Syrup to taste

Shake with ice.

BACARDI

2 oz. light Bacardi (Rum)
2 tsp. Lime Juice
1/2 tsp. superfine Sugar
1 dash Grenadine to each drink

Shake with ice. This is a pink Rum Sour or Daiquiri, but by court ruling a bartender must use Bacardi rum when asked for a "Bacardi."

BLACK RUSSIAN

2 oz. Vodka
1 oz. Kahlua

Mix Vodka and Kahlua over ice. Stir. For White Russian, add 1/2 oz. cream.

BLOODY MARY

3 oz. Tomato Juice
1-1/2 oz. Vodka

1 tsp. Lemon Juice
1 dash Worcestershire and Tabasco Sauce
Pepper to taste

Shake with ice, and serve in a highball glass.

BLOODY MARIA

Substitute tequila for vodka in a regular Bloody Mary.

BRONX

1-1/2 oz. Gin
2 tsp. Italian (sweet) Vermouth
2 tsp. French (dry) Vermouth
2 tsp. Orange Juice
1 oz. Lemon Juice

Shake with ice. Put a twist of orange peel in each glass.

BRANDY COCKTAIL

2 oz. Brandy
1/2 tsp. Curacao
1 Lemon Peel
1 dash Bitters
1/2 tsp. Sugar

Shake with ice. Add a twist of lemon peel to each glass. Other brandy cocktails are given the same name.

BRANDY SMASH

Muddle 2-3 sprigs of mint, and 1/2 teaspoon sugar in an Old-Fashioned glass. Put in 2 cubes of ice, and add 2 ounces of brandy. Stir slightly.

11

CAPTAIN'S BLOOD

3 oz. Jamaica Rum
1 oz. Lime Juice
2 dashes Bitters per drink

Shake with ice.

CHAMPAGNE COCKTAIL

In a champagne glass, soak a piece of lump sugar, or a teaspoonful of granulated sugar, with a few dashes of bitters. Fill with chilled champagne, and drop in twist of lemon peel, or float some heavy rum on top of drink.

CHICAGO

1-1/2 oz. Brandy
2 dashes Curacao or Triple Sec
1 dash Bitters
Champagne (to be added)

Stir with ice, and pour into chilled and frosted champagne glass. Fill with chilled champagne.

CLOVER CLUB

6 parts Gin
2 parts Lemon Juice
1 part Grenadine or Raspberry Syrup
1 Egg White to each 2 drinks

Shake all ingredients except gin with cracked ice. Add half the gin, and shake again. Add balance of gin, shake, and strain.

A glistening white Christmas
With snow on the trees,
Makes appetites hearty
And easy to please!

CUBA LIBRE

2 oz. Light Rum
Juice of half a Lemon or Lime
Coca-Cola
3 ice cubes

In a highball glass add rum, lemon and ice. Fill
with Cola and stir.

DAIQUIRI

2 oz. White Label Rum
2 tsp. Lime Juice
1/2 tsp. superfine Sugar

Shake with ice. This is a Rum Sour or unpink-
ened Bacardi under its more common name.

FROZEN DAIQUIRI

4-6 oz. Rum
1 packet Sour or Collins Mix
Ice
1/2 Banana (Strawberries or Blueberries can
  be substituted)

Pour rum into blender. Add sour or collins mix
and ice, followed by desired fruit. Blend.

DUBONNET COCKTAIL

1-1/4 oz. Gin
1-1/4 oz. Dubonnet

Stir with ice. Drop twisted lemon peel in drink.

FALERNUM COCKTAIL

2 parts White or Gold Label Rum
1 part Jamaica Rum
1 part Lemon Juice
1/3 part Falernum
1 dash Bitters for each drink

Shake with ice. Falernum has an almond flavor.

GIBSON

A Martini with a small pickled cocktail onion
instead of an olive.

GIN AND IT

1-1/2 oz. Gin (or more)
1 oz. Italian (sweet) Vermouth

Stir with ice. Add twist of lemon peel. Can be
made on-the-rocks in Old-Fashioned glass.

GIN AND BITTERS

Shake 4-5 dashes bitters into Old-Fashioned glass. Add 2 cubes of ice, and 2 ounces or more of gin. Stir slightly.

GIMLET DRY

2 oz. Gin
2 tsp. Rose's Lime Juice

Stir with ice. A tart dry summer cocktail, to which many drinkers will want to add a little sugar syrup.

GRASSHOPPER

1 oz. green Creme de Menthe
1 oz. white Creme de Cacao
1 oz. Cream
Ice

Pour Creme de Menthe, Creme De Cacao, and Cream into a shaker. Add ice, shake, and strain into a cocktail glass.

HARVEY WALLBANGER

1-1/2 oz. Vodka
4 oz. Orange Juice
1/2 oz. Galliano Liqueur

Fill half a 10-ounce glass with ice cubes. Pour vodka and orange juice over ice. Float Galliano on top.

MARTINI ON THE ROCKS

Shake or stir ingredients with ice, and pour over 2 ice cubes in an Old-Fashioned glass. If the liquors are not chilled first, too much ice in the glass will melt. Twist lemon peel over drink, and drop in.

MANHATTAN

2-1/2 oz. Rye
1 oz. Italian (sweet) Vermouth
1 dash Bitters

Stir with ice. Serve with maraschino cherry with stem or on toothpick. Like the Martini, this is all liquor.

MANHATTAN VARIATIONS

You can add some lemon or pineapple juice to an ordinary Manhattan, and get a pleasant cocktail, or you can add almost any of the pungent liqueurs (a few dashes only) for aromatic variations. And of course brandy, rum or other liquors can substitute for rye or bourbon.

MARGARITA

4 oz. Tequila
4 oz. Triple Sec
1 can frozen Lime Juice (6 oz. size)
Ice

Pour tequila, Triple Sec and lime juice into a blender. Add ice and blend. If desired, rim glasses with salt and serve.

MIMOSA

1 part Champagne
1 part Orange Juice
Triple Sec
Orange Wheel

Mix chilled champagne and orange juice in large
champagne glass. Add dash of Triple Sec and
garnish with orange wheel.

OLD-FASHIONED

Into each Old-Fashioned glass put 1 teaspoon
sugar syrup and 2 dashes bitters. Blend with
spoon, add 1 ounce rye or bourbon whiskey,
and blend again. Put in 2 cubes of ice, cracked,
and add 1 ounce (or more) whiskey. Stir. Twist
lemon peel over drink, and drop in; decorate
with maraschino cherry. If no syrup is available,
use sugar with just enough water to dissolve it.
For light drinkers, garnishing with pineapple,
orange slice, etc. is gracious; most drinkers prefer
just the lemon peel and a cherry.

ORANGE BLOSSOM

1-1/2 oz. Gin
1-1/2 oz. Orange Juice
1/2 tsp. superfine Sugar

Shake with ice. Garnish glass with small twist
of orange peel.

PINK LADY

1 oz. Gin
1/2 oz. Apple Brandy

1/2 oz. Lemon or Lime Juice
1 tsp. Grenadine
1 Egg White for each 2 drinks

Shake the non-alcoholic ingredients thoroughly
with ice. Then add half the liquors, and shake.
Add the balance, and shake once more.

PINA COLADA

4-6 oz. Rum
7 oz. Coconut Cream
10 oz. Pineapple Juice
Ice
Cherry and Pineapple Chunks

Pour rum, coconut cream, and pineapple juice
into blender. Add ice, preferably in small cubes
or shaved. Blend. Garnish with a cherry and
pineapple chunk on cocktail toothpick.

PLANTER'S PUNCH

2 oz. Rum
1 oz. Jamaica Rum
Juice from one Lime
1 tsp. Sugar
Club Soda

Mix rum, Jamaica Rum, lime juice, and sugar in
cocktail glass. Add ice, fill with soda and stir.

ROB ROY

2 parts Scotch whisky
1 part Italian (sweet) Vermouth
1 dash bitters.

Stir with ice.

God rest you merry, Gentlemen!

SAZERAC

2 oz. Whiskey
1 tsp. Sugar Syrup
3 dashes Orange or Angostura Bitters
2 dashes Absinthe (Pernod)

Stir with ice cubes, and pour into thoroughly chilled Old-Fashioned glass.

SIDE CAR

2 oz. Brandy
2 tsp. Lemon Juice
2 tsp. Cointreau or Triple Sec

Shake with ice. Twist a piece of lemon peel over drink and drop in.

SCREWDRIVER

Put ice and 2 ounces Vodka in a highball glass. Full with orange juice. Stir.

SLOE COMFORTABLE SCREW

1-1/2 oz. Vodka
1 oz. Sloe Gin
1-1/2 oz. Southern Comfort
Orange Juice

Pour in a highball glass filled with ice. Stir.

SPRITZER

1 part Rhine Wine
1 part Club Soda

Mix wine and soda over ice. Stir and garnish with a lemon twist.

TEQUILA SUNRISE

1-1/2 oz. Tequila
1/2 oz. Grenadine
Orange Juice

In a highball glass filled with ice, pour tequila, Grenadine, and orange juice. Do not stir, but add a straw.

TOASTED ALMOND

1-1/2 oz. Kahlua
1 oz. Amaretto
Milk

Pour Kahlua and Amaretto over ice in a highball glass. Fill with milk and stir.

TOM COLLINS

2 oz. Gin
Juice from 1/2 Lemon
1 tsp. sugar
Club Soda
Lemon or Lime garnish

Mix gin, lemon juice, and sugar in cocktail glass.
Add ice and soda. Stir. Serve with desired garnish.

VERMOUTH CASSIS

3 oz. French (dry) Vermouth
1 oz. Creme de Cassis

Usually served in a tall glass, with soda and ice;
but may also be served, stirred with ice, as a
cocktail.

VODKA GIBSON

2-1/2 oz. Vodka
1 Tbs. French (dry) Vermouth

Stir with ice, and strain. Add cocktail onion.

WHISKEY SOUR

2 oz. Whiskey
1 oz. Lemon Juice
1 Tbs. Sugar Syrup

Shake with ice. This is a true before-dinner
cocktail, like the Daiquiri. The usual Sour, a
good afternoon drink, has a higher proportion
of lemon juice and sugar, and should be deco-
rated with fruit.

FRAPPÉS

Fill a champagne glass with shaved ice. Into it pour a jigger of Absinthe (Pernod) or Creme de Menthe.

WITCH'S TWITCH

1-1/2 oz. White Rum
2 tsp. White Creme de Cacao
2 tsp. Triple Sec
1 Tbs. Heavy Cream
4 oz. Chilled Club Soda
1/2 Small Lime
Ground Cinnamon
Nutmeg

In a highball glass with 5 ice cubes, put rum, creme de cacao and triple sec. Stir. Squeeze 1/2 lime over drink, and add to drink. Add soda; stir. Sprinkle cinnamon and nutmeg on top.

HOT TODDIES
& MULLED WINES

HOT DRINKS *no longer have the same appeal for us that they had for earlier generations — living as we do in steam-heated houses and apartments. Gone are the days when a piping hot bowl of Christmas Wassail gave warmth to the Christmas party in drafty Bracebridge Hall as described by Washington Irving. And gone are the days when a hot grog was a necessary potion for a New England farmer (and his wife) just before they went upstairs to their icy bedroom on Christmas Eve.*

Nevertheless there are times and places when hot drinks are mighty good. Skiing and skating parties; Christmas-weeks at country houses which never warm up like an apartment; cold nights in Autumn, too early to start the furnace. At such times, remember these recipes!

OLDE YULE WASSAIL

Heat 1 quart ale almost to boiling point. Into it stir some grated nutmeg, powdered ginger, and grated peel of one lemon. While ale is heating, beat up 3 eggs with 4 ounces of moistened white sugar.

Put hot ale into beaten sugar and eggs in one pitcher, and into another put 1 quart of warmed rum or brandy. Turn ingredients from one pitcher into the other until mixture is smooth, then pour into holly-wreathed Wassail Bowl.

Use hot pitchers and a pre-heated Wassail Bowl. Be sure the drink is hot! 24 three-ounce servings.

HOT TODDY

1 teaspoon Sugar
Small piece of Cinnamon
Slices of Lemon garnished with Cloves
1½ ounces Rye or Brandy
Boiling Water

Put a spoon of sugar in an Old-Fashioned glass; dissolve it with a little hot water, and leave spoon in glass. Add the cinnamon, lemon, and whiskey and fill the glass nearly full with piping hot water. Stir gently. Grate a little nutmeg on top and serve.

HOT BUTTERED RUM

2 dashes Bitters
3 ounces dark Rum
1 teaspoon Butter
3 or 4 Cloves
Boiling Water

Dash the bitters into a glass or pewter mug. Add the rum and place a teaspoon with the butter in the rum. Pour piping hot water into the mug. Sprinkle a few cloves on top. Stir with the spoon and allow to steep for a few minutes.

HOT TOM AND JERRY

For two 6-ounce servings:

1 Egg, separated
2 ounces Gold Label Rum
1 ounce Brandy or Whiskey
2 teaspoons Sugar
6 ounces Hot Milk

Beat egg yolk, adding sugar. Stir in liquor, then egg white, well beaten. Pour into glasses or mugs, adding hot milk. Sprinkle with grated nutmeg.

FARMER'S BISHOP

Select 6 oranges with nice peels. Stick each with 8 cloves, and bake them whole in a slow oven for 1 hour. Place them in a heated punch bowl, and prick well with a fork. Pour over them 1 quart slightly heated apple brandy, and sprinkle with 2 tablespoons sugar. Set fire to the brandy, letting it burn for a few seconds only, then extinguish the flame by pouring over it ½ gallon almost boiling cider, reserving ½ cup of cider. Into this ½ cup stir beforehand the following: 1 teaspoon ground cinnamon, ¼ teaspoon ground nutmeg. Add this mixture to the hot prepared punchbowl with more sugar if you want. Serve at once. Reheat bowl contents in a chafing dish, or over the stove, as needed, for refills. Makes 32 three-ounce servings.

GLOG

Into a large casserole put 1 ounce bitters, ¾ cup granulated sugar, 1 pint claret, 1 pint sherry, ½ pint brandy. Place over fire until piping hot. For each serving put 1 large raisin and 1 unsalted almond in an Old-Fashioned glass and fill glass ¾ full. Or use punch glasses. (A spoon in the glass before pouring in the hot liquid prevents the glass from cracking). 14 three-ounce servings.

Ring in the new,
Ring out the old,
A steaming hot toddy
Will cure a bad cold!

HOT SPICED APPLE CIDER

2 quarts Sweet Apple Cider
8 ounces White or Gold Label Rum
Few Sticks Cinnamon

Heat cider with cinnamon sticks. Add rum before serving. Rum content can be considerably increased; or you can pour varying amounts (up to 1 ounce) in each glass before adding hot cider. Use wine glasses or punch goblets. 24 three-ounce servings.

29

HOT FRUITED CIDER

2 quarts Sweet Apple Cider
1 pint Grapefruit Juice (unsweetened)
½ cup Brown Sugar
Few Sticks Cinnamon
1 pint Light Rum

Put all ingredients except rum into large sauce-pan and bring to a low boil for a few minutes. Strain into serving pitcher and add to punch-cups or wine-glasses which have been prepared with ½ to 1 ounce of rum. Pre-heat pitcher if there is any danger of cracking from heat. 30 three-ounce servings.

HOT SPICED CRANBERRY PUNCH

¾ cup Brown Sugar, firmly packed
4 cups Water
¼ teaspoon Salt
¼ teaspoon Nutmeg
½ teaspoon Cinnamon
½ teaspoon Allspice
¾ teaspoon Cloves
2 cans jellied Cranberry Sauce
1 quart Pineapple Juice
1 pint Rum
Cinnamon Sticks
Butter

Bring to a boil sugar, 1 cup water, salt, spices. Crush cranberry sauce with fork. Add water and beat with rotary beater until smooth. Add cranberry liquid and pineapple juice to hot spiced syrup and heat to boiling. Add rum. Serve hot. Dot with butter. Serve with cinnamon stick stirrers. 35 three-ounce servings.

MULLED WINE

Peel of ½ Lemon, cut into curls
Peel of ½ Orange, cut into curls
6 lumps Sugar
1 teaspoon Allspice
2 teaspoons Cinnamon
2 teaspoons ground Cloves
3 cups boiling Water
2 quarts, Sherry, Marsala, or Burgundy

Pour boiling water over the fruit peel, sugar, and spices and simmer for 10 minutes. Place in a punchbowl. Add the wine, which has been heated to the boiling point but not allowed to boil. In merrie Old England, a poker was heated in the fire-place, and thrust into the bowl. 30 three-ounce servings.

HOT GROG

This is a Rum Toddy. Put a spoon of sugar, a slice of lemon with a clove, and 1½ ounces of rum in an Old-Fashioned glass or mug. Leave spoon in glass to prevent cracking. Pour in boiling water, and stir to dissolve the sugar.

HOT MILK PUNCH

Put a spoon of sugar and 1½ ounces rum in a tumbler. Keep spoon in glass to avoid cracking. Add hot (unboiled) milk to fill glass, and stir.

WINE FACTS AND USE

Here are a few basic facts and rules about wine. There are three kinds of wines: Fortified, Sparkling and Table Wines.

FORTIFIED WINES

Fortified wines have a high alcoholic content: 20 percent or more — nearly half that of straight whiskies and other hard liquors.

The common fortified wines are Sherry and Port.

SHERRY derives its name from Jerez in Spain. It is also called Sack, probably from *seco* or dry. Part of the payment of the English Poet-Laureate is in "Sack."

The new wine of the Jerez area of Spain, as it ferments, is "fortified" by adding some local brandy to it, and is then allowed to stand, exposed to the air, while it slowly turns into sherry. At the end of a year, each cask is checked as to its quality and type, and brought to a warehouse with many other casks. There the current bottling is produced by blending older with newer wines. By judicious selection from the always-large supply, flavor, color and quality are made uniform under each label. There are no vintage years in sherry, but there are stable variations of flavor and quality.

The usual kinds of Sherry:

Fino, pale and dry, to be served cold as an appetizer before meals.

AMONTILLADO, dry, but darker than Fino. Also may be served cold as an appetizer.

OLOROSO and AMOROSO, both medium-sweet and medium-heavy. Serve at room temperature.

GOLDEN, BROWN, or SOLERA, heavy, sweet, and dark. Serve at room temperature.

The sweet fortified wines (Port, Tokay, Marsala, and the sweeter Sherries and Madeira) are *not* appetizers or dinner wines. They are dessert or after-dinner wines, being too sweet and heavy to serve with the meal. Serve at room temperature.

PORT derives its name from Portugal, its country of origin. But no Port is drunk in Portugal — it is all shipped to England and America.

As in the making of sherry, so in making port — some local brandy is added to the fermenting wine. This extra alcohol, by bringing the brew to a stable alcoholic content, forestalls the conversion of all the grape sugar into alcohol. Thus port (like sherry) is both sweeter and stronger than ordinary wines in which the fermentation is allowed to complete itself naturally.

The best of each year's making is set aside for aging as "Vintage" Port. The rest is blended; so that — as in sherry — the quality under any one label is likely to be uniform.

TAWNY PORT is aged in wood, is lighter in flavor and is the least alcoholic.

RUBY PORT is a blend of Tawny and new red wines.

VINTAGE PORT is the best of the year's crop, aged in the bottle from 15 to 40 years, and therefore expensive.

CRUSTED PORT is a blend of Vintage Ports, aged in the cask; its name comes from the "crust" or heavy deposit it casts in the bottle. It must be moved and decanted with great care before serving.

CHAMPAGNE AND OTHER SPARKLING WINES

Champagne is the greatest sparkling wine, but all others have the same usage.

Champagnes are festive, and properly belong at holiday parties, weddings, and other celebrations. They may be served as appetizers (plain or as champagne cocktails), or with the meal, preferably with lobster, poultry or other white meat.

Always chill champagne bottles before opening. Use refrigerator, ice-bucket, or snow, and be sure the chilling is thoroughly done. An un-chilled bottle is sure to make trouble when you open it. Putting ice-cubes in the glass is *not* the way to chill champagne, or any other wine.

To open a bottle of chilled champagne: Remove foil, and hold the bottle up at a 45-degree angle, facing away from you. Untwist the wire and remove it, and then gently *turn* (do not pull!) the cork. Turning loosens the cork, and internal pressure in the bottle pushes it out —

I drove my Reindeer to the market,
And friendly neighbors helped me park it!

so, while turning the cork, you must hold it
back against the pressure. Properly opened, a
champagne bottle puffs, it does not pop.

Champagnes vary from semi-sweetness to dry-
ness in this order: Doux, Sec, Extra Dry, Brut.

Champagne cannot be kept after it is opened.
So be sure to finish the bottle! Splits (small
bottles) should be used when two people want
a modest quantity each.

To make a Champagne Cocktail: in a champagne glass put a level teaspoon of sugar, or a

small lump of sugar. Impregnate with 2 or 3 dashes Bitters. Add *chilled* champagne to fill a small glass, ⅔ fill a large one.

TABLE WINES

WHITE WINES come both sweet and dry. They should be served *chilled*, in plain white stemware, so the color of the wine can be seen. (Rhine wine is sometimes served in green glassware.)

SWEET WHITE WINES are Sauternes, Barsac, and (very sweet) Haute Sauternes, from the Bordeaux district in France — or from domestic vineyards using similar grapes and similar methods. Such sweet wines are best with poultry or dessert.

DRY WHITE WINES are usually Graves (Bordeaux), White Burgundy, Chablis, Rhine, or Moselle — if European; or are from domestic vineyards growing similar grapes. They are excellent and proper with fish, poultry, and light meats like lamb, pork and veal.

ROSÉ OR PINK WINES are dry, and served chilled like white wines. They are especially suited to light meats.

RED WINES are always dry, are always served at room temperature, and are most suitable to serve with red meats. Claret (Red Bordeaux) and Chianti are rather light-bodied; Burgundy is heavy-bodied and is especially appropriate with steak and beef. Beaujolais, though not technically a Burgundy, comes from the same area and has the same general characteristics.

Plain clear stemware is best for serving all table wines.

OTHER WINE POINTERS

Until used, all wine bottles should be stored in a cool place on their sides (to keep the corks immersed and damp). Red wines should be uncorked, and stood upright, an hour or so before serving, so that any sediment can settle.

Chill white wines in the bottle — using your refrigerator, ice-bucket, or snow — never by using ice cubes in the glass.

It is wise to uncork white wines too, beforehand, (or any wine except Champagne and other sparkling wines), as a precaution against a difficult or broken cork. (Work around it with a narrow-bladed knife — but be careful of your other hand!) If a cork is hopelessly broken or stuck, you will have to dig it out and push part of it in — in which case decant into a glass pitcher or another clean bottle, to serve from.

Be sure to have on hand a good corkscrew: one which exerts leverage to draw the cork two-thirds of the way out. Your final pull will then be easy, and there will be no splashing on the floor or table-cloth.

After drawing cork from a wine bottle wipe the top and inside lip to remove cork fragments, and serve a quarter-glass to yourself first, to make sure any cork fragments inside the bottle do not get into a guest's glass. Fill up your own glass after the others have been served.

Remember that a red wine of any age, particularly a Burgundy, can have a good deal of sediment. Decanting, and the actual pouring, will have to be done gently; and the bottom inch of the bottle is best left unpoured if it is dirty.

Allow some time for red wine to settle after decanting.

When serving wine a napkin around the bottle will catch any drippings; but if you are proud of the label you will show it and let the drippings (if any) fall if they will!

Fill glasses about two-thirds full, so the aroma is trapped in the top of the glass when the wine is sipped.

Open bottles of fortified wines can be kept indefinitely at room temperature without spoiling.

Open bottles of white wine can be kept a week or more (in the refrigerator) without spoiling.

Open bottles of red wine can be kept a week or more at room temperature without spoiling.

AFTER DINNER
CHEER

BRANDIES, CORDIALS, LIQUEURS

After a heavy meal a tiny strong drink is often pleasanter than a long drink, and is an aid to digestion. There are three types of such liquor: brandies, cordials, liqueurs.

BRANDIES are made by distilling wine. They are therefore very strong alcoholically, and yet delicate in flavor. They are usually served either in small pony glasses or in "snifters" — large tulip-shaped glasses in which one ounce or so of brandy is swirled around and warmed by the hands of the connoisseur who savors the fumes before he tastes.

The best and most famous brandy is Cognac, from the little French city of that name. By French law, only brandies made from grapes grown in two French *départements* are entitled to use the "Cognac" name.

The French government carefully controls the manufacture of this brandy — and taxes each liter of it. Each vineyard owner has his wine-vats measured and checked after each wine-making, and receives a license to distill the amount of wine he has on hand, and no more. The individual distillations — at this point very raw and pale — are sold to the large brandy merchants in the town, in whose cellars the liquor in the casks will age, evaporate, and darken until it is ready to be blended and bottled for commerce.

Raw grape brandy is 70% alcohol (140 proof). It takes perhaps 40 years for it to reduce itself to 100 proof, at which point it is possible to drink. Obviously 40 years is too long for a brandy dealer to wait for his investment to mature: so at the end of ten years or so the brandy is diluted with water, darkened with caramel, and bottled with an impressive label. All brandies under 25 years of age are so diluted; probably most 25-year brandies are diluted also. Obviously any brandy which really is kept in cask about 50 years to be fully matured, and only then bottled, must be sold at a high price.

The brandy of Armagnac ranks next to Cognac. Some Spanish brandy is excellent. In general, other brandies should be used in mixed drinks only (if at all). Cognac of a good house, and as old as possible, should be reserved for after-dinner satisfaction.

Brandy does not improve in the bottle, only in the original cask. Keeping a bottle of brandy for years will not age it, and probably will harm it. Brandy in an opened bottle will not keep as well as in a sealed unopened bottle.

Apple brandy — or applejack as it is commonly and not quite correctly called — can be a very crude and powerful drink when it is young; just like grape brandy. Applejack really is a distillation from an apple mash. Apple brandy is a distillation from hard cider — cider which has already fermented, just as grapes have fermented in the making of wine.

Apple brandy ages slowly, like grape brandy. The Calvados from France is a superior apple brandy properly prepared, and is as expensive as a cognac of equal quality. Kirsch is Cherry Brandy — again properly prepared.

CORDIALS. In this country "Cherry Brandy" or "Apricot Brandy" or similar titles usually refer to a cherry- or apricot-flavored grain alcohol; sometimes to a flavored brandy. Such liquors are more properly titled "Cordials." True brandy is never sweet; and never has more than a faint memory-flavor of its original fruit.

Cordials make excellent after-dinner drinks, being at once strong and sweet. Serve in pony glasses or little liqueur glasses.

LIQUEURS are sweet, powerfully alcoholic delicacies made (usually by secret formulas) from infusions of many herbs and spices. Serve in pony glasses or little liqueur glasses.

Some famous varieties of liqueurs:

Benedictine	Crème de Menthe
B & B (Benedictine and Brandy)	Curacao
	Grand Marnier
Chartreuse	Kummel
Cointreau	Strega
Crème de Cacao	Triple Sec

Liqueurs are often used as ingredients in cocktails. They may be used as frappés (pour over shaved ice in cocktail glass; serve with short straws).

Let's drink and be merry
For tomorrow we die;
And today seems far brighter
With a bottle of rye!

APÉRITIF WINES AND APPETIZERS

Apéritifs which may be drunk straight (and chilled) include dry Sherry, dry Madeira, Vermouth, Dubonnet, and Pernod.

Vermouth is a fortified white wine which has been made much as sherry is made, and to which aromatic spices have been added. The dry vermouth of France is an excellent mixer (as in the Martini) but it may be drunk straight or in other ways. The sweeter vermouth from Italy is best used as a mixer (as in the Manhattan). The fact that vermouth is made like sherry suggests

45

that a dry sherry makes a fair substitute for French vermouth in a Martini, and a sweet sherry for Italian vermouth in a Manhattan.

Absinthe is a supposedly-poisonous aromatic wine which by law is no longer manufactured here or abroad. Its place has been taken by substitutes (Pernod is the standard brand) which have the same green color, the same flavor derived from wormwood and anise — and which remain popular drinks in Parisian sidewalk cafés.

Dubonnet is another *apéritif* popular in France. It is an aromatic wine like Vermouth and Pernod, but sweeter in flavor.

FRAPPÉS

Dubonnet, Pernod, Vermouth — as well as the popular Crème de Menthe — are excellent in the form of frappés. Fill a champagne glass or Old-Fashioned glass with shaved ice, and pour over it 1½ ounces of the liquor. Serve with short straw.

SCOTCH MIST

Pour a jigger of Scotch into an Old-Fashioned glass filled with shaved ice. Add a twist of lemon peel.

ABOUT INGREDIENTS

Use good ingredients. If you want to buy cheaper grades of liquor which often taste just as good as more expensive ones, get advice from a dependable dealer. But to be perfectly safe, buy a better brand of a reliable house. The cost per drink is not much greater with a better grade of liquor.

GIN. This is a redistillation of raw alcohol to which juniper berries and other flavoring herbs have been added. It is clear, colorless, and delicately aromatic — when properly made. Aged gin (the yellow variety) is blander, better, and costlier, but it destroys the water-pale look currently popular in Martinis.

"Hollands" Gin and Sloe Gin can *not* be substituted for the usual variety if you want the usual results. "Old Tom" Gin is sweetened. It may be used in a Tom Collins (to which it gave its name) — in which case do not add any other sweetening. "Old Tom" can *not* be used in a Martini or other "dry" cocktail, or in Gin-and-Tonic.

RUM. This is a liquor made from sugar cane molasses, chiefly in the Caribbean. There are three varieties. White Label is clear, light, delicate-flavored, Gold Label is somewhat darker and with more flavor; these come from Cuba (the best), Puerto Rico, or the Virgin Islands. The third variety is the dark, heavy, Tropical rum, from which the molasses flavor has not been filtered, and which usually comes from

47

ON MAKING PUNCHES

PUNCHES are made with a block of ice (or a big bucketful of cubes) in a punchbowl. They are an ideal means of serving a large crowd. It is better, in preparing to make a punch, to freeze some trays of water *without* the cube dividers. The solid block will not melt so fast as cubes.

A PUNCH CUP or Wine Cup is the same sort of beverage on a small scale, using a few ice-cubes in a pitcher.

Like other mixed drinks, punches should be adapted to the kind of people you are entertaining. A country-club or sophisticated crowd can take a well-spiked punch, and such a drink will certainly enliven your party. A church group or a young people's group may *like* to be told that they are being devilish and drinking hard liquor — but it will be well to use fruit juices and pop soda and white wine for the main body of your drink, and to keep the strong alcoholic ingredients to a minimum.

A punch is always a sweet drink; but if it is served before a meal it should be as close to tartness as you dare. A really sweet drink before a meal spoils the enjoyment of soup or most other first courses; it is not an appetizer.

All of the punches which follow are built on a similar pattern: first, fruit juices and flavorings; then up to 25% hard liquor and up to 50% wine; and the balance soda water, tea, apple cider, etc. You can safely make your own formula if you will avoid two pitfalls in the hard liquor department: 1. Never use Scotch, which is a bad mixer; and 2. If you use gin, use no other hard liquor in combination with it, and remember that gin mixes best with citrus fruits. Other liquors: brandy, rye, bourbon and rum, will mix with any fruit — and with each other — and with wine.

Any punch can be made more potent by reducing the quantity of soda or tea or water it contains. Any punch can be made less potent by adding soda, ginger ale, apple cider, or tea.

Apple cider is a neglected ingredient in most punches. But it is an inexpensive and highly useful fruit juice. Grape juice has a distinctive flavor, but it makes for a red punch. Generally a lighter-color punch is preferred.

Champagne or other sparkling wine in a punch prepared in the *kitchen* is a waste: soda water gives the same bubbles. But champagne added in public is a festive gesture. *Be sure the bottle is chilled before opening.* See page 36. Sparkling Grape Juice — if available — is a delicious non-alcoholic beverage like sweet champagne, and is a perfect substitute for champagne.

Always garnish your punchbowl with sliced fruit, cherries, etc. Cucumber slices and melon balls are excellent additions.

Punch is usually served in small goblets or glass cups — 3 to 4 ounces per serving.

Gold or white label rum may be used interchangeably. Sparkling white burgundy can be substituted for champagne.

Party Punch Bowls

ANTOINE'S CHAMPAGNE PUNCH

2 ounces Maraschino Syrup or Liqueur
2 ounces Cointreau, Curacao or Triple Sec
5 ounces Brandy
4 ounces Sugar Syrup
1 bottle Sauterne
1 pint Club Soda
1 quart chilled Champagne

Garnish with fresh pineapple, peeled orange slices, and the cherries from the maraschino syrup. 30 three-ounce servings. A strong drink.

APRICOT BUBBLES

1 large can (46 oz.) Apricot Nectar
2 cans Frozen Orange Juice
1 can Frozen Lemon Juice (unsweetened)
1 can (18 oz.) Pineapple Juice
1 bottle Sauterne
1 bottle Light Rum
2 bottles Lemon or Lime Soda

Allow frozen juices to melt; then mix all ingredients with ice in punchbowl — adding soda at the last moment. Decorate with fruit slices, maraschino cherries, strawberries, etc. 60 three-ounce servings.

With this large quantity of fruit juice, more liquor can well be added to make a more potent drink.

A toast to St. Nick!

ARTILLERY PUNCH

¾ cup Sugar
6 ounces Lemon Juice
1 tablespoon Bitters
1 bottle Red Wine
1 bottle Sherry
1 bottle Rye or Bourbon
1 bottle Brandy
1 quart Club Soda

Mix sugar and lemon juice and let stand for an hour. Add to liquors and stir in bowl with ice, then add club soda just before serving. 32 powerful three-ounce servings.

BOMBAY PUNCH

3 ounces Maraschino Syrup or Liqueur
3 ounces Apricot Cordial
3 ounces Curacao or Cointreau

53

1 quart Club Soda
1 pint Sherry
1 pint Brandy
2 bottles chilled Champagne or Ginger Ale

Pour into punch bowl with a large block of ice. Garnish with slices of fresh fruit and sprigs of mint. Add champagne last, just before serving. 42 three-ounce servings.

BRANDY PUNCH

6 ounces Lemon Juice
6 ounces Orange Juice
4 ounces Curacao, Triple Sec or Cointreau
2 ounces Grenadine
1 bottle Brandy
1 quart Club Soda

Dissolve sugar in juices beforehand. Pour ingredients over ice, stir, and add soda water just before serving. 35 three-ounce servings.

CHAMPAGNE PUNCH

4 ounces Lemon Juice
4 ounces Pineapple Juice
3 ounces Grenadine or Maraschino Syrup
3 ounces Fruit Cordial
8 ounces Brandy
1 bottle White Wine
2 bottles chilled Champagne

Pour all ingredients except champagne over ice, stir, and add champagne just before serving. Garnish bowl with fruit slices and strawberries. 32 powerful three-ounce servings.

CHAMPAGNE STRAWBERRY PUNCH

2 packages frozen sliced Peaches
  or Pineapple chunks
1 Lemon, sliced thin
½ package Strawberries
1 bottle Sauterne
6 ounces Brandy
3 bottles chilled Champagne

Allow fruit to defrost 2 hours in small bowl, with lemon juices. (Add extra lemon juice if pineapple is used). Pour over ice, add brandy, and stir. Add chilled champagne just before serving in glasses garnished with peach slice. 42 strong three-ounce servings.

EGG NOG

12 Eggs, separated
8 ounces Sugar
1 quart Heavy Cream
1 quart Milk
1 quart Whiskey
8 ounces Jamaica Rum

Beat egg yolks with sugar until dissolved. Add liquor, milk, and cream, and then egg-whites stiffly beaten. Chill in refrigerator for a couple of hours or more, before serving with grated nutmeg. 40-50 servings.

The liquor, milk, and sugar content can be varied greatly to suit your taste. Either rye or bourbon whiskey can be used, and brandy is often substituted for the rum. The egg-yolks may be added just before serving — in which case they should be sweetened slightly.

COFFEE EGG NOG

Make like regular Egg Nog, substituting 1 quart cold strong coffee for the milk. Depending on your taste, you will have to add a little or large quantity of sugar to sweeten the coffee.

FISH HOUSE PUNCH

6 ounces Sugar Syrup
1½ pints Lemon juice
1 bottle White Label Rum
1 bottle Jamaica Rum
1 bottle Brandy
8 ounces Peach Cordial
2 bottles Club Soda

Let all ingredients (except soda water) stand for 2 or 3 hours. Before serving, pour over ice in bowl, and add soda. Makes 50 three-ounce servings. This powerful punch was reportedly very popular in American Revolutionary days.

GIN PUNCH

8 ounces Lemon Juice, unsweetened
1 quart Orange Juice
4 ounces Grenadine
1 bottle Gin
1 bottle Club Soda

Pour over block of ice, or a heap of ice cubes. Add the soda last. Garnish with fruit slices and mint. 30 three-ounce servings.

Fine wines aid the digestion!

HOT RUM PUNCH

6 Lemons, grated and juiced
6 ounces Sugar
2 teaspoons ground Ginger
1 bottle Gold Label Rum
1 bottle Brandy
8 ounces Sherry
1½ quarts boiling Water

Mix and muddle sugar, ginger, and lemon gratings and juice. Let stand for an hour or more. Put into large bowl, and add enough hot water to cover. Stir thoroughly, and add liquors and balance of hot water. 32 three-ounce servings.

Warmed punch goblets are a nicety in serving a hot punch.

[*For additional hot drinks turn to page 26*]

57

HARVEST PUNCH

2 quarts Sweet Apple Cider
1 bottle White Wine
½ bottle Gin
2 ounces Orange Cordial or other fruit flavor

Garnish with fruit slices (including thin cucumber slices) and strawberries. A different punch from the ordinary, and an excellent one. 30 three-ounce servings.

LAFAYETTE PUNCH

6 Oranges
½ pound Sugar
2 bottles Rhine Wine
3 quarts Champagne, iced

Slice the oranges, arrange them on the bottom of the punchbowl, and sprinkle with sugar. Let stand at least an hour, adding 1 bottle of wine after the sugar begins to soak up the juices. When ready to serve, add ice to bowl, then remaining bottle of wine and the chilled champagne. 60 three-ounce servings.

MERCURIO PUNCH

1 quart Grape Juice
1 bottle Red Wine
1 bottle White Wine
1 pint Brandy or Rum
6 ounces Benedictine (or Curacao, Triple Sec, Grand Marnier)
1 bottle Club Soda or Champagne
½ pound Sugar

Dissolve sugar in grape juice. When thoroughly dissolved, pour into punchbowl with balance of ingredients — the club soda last. Garnish with fruit slices. 44 three-ounce servings.

PINEAPPLE CHAMPAGNE

3 Ripe Pineapples
1 pound Powdered Sugar
1 pint Lemon Juice
4 ounces Maraschino
4 ounces Curacao or Triple Sec
1 pint Brandy
1 pint Jamaica Rum
4 quarts Champagne, iced

Peel, slice and crush the pineapple, cover with sugar, and let stand 2 hours. Add all other ingredients except champagne, stir, and let stand (covered) overnight. Pour over ice when ready to serve, and add champagne. 70 three-ounce servings — strong ones!

ROMAN PUNCH

6 ounces Lemon Juice
6 ounces Orange Juice
½ pound Sugar
6 Eggs (whites only)
1 bottle Gold Label Rum
2 ounces Bitters
1 bottle Club Soda
1 bottle Champagne

Dissolve sugar in fruit juice, add bitters, and

let stand till thoroughly blended. When ready to serve, beat whites of eggs thoroughly; add with rum and carbonated water. Add champagne, well-chilled, at the table. 32 three-ounce servings.

ST. LOUIS PUNCH

¼ pound candied Pineapple
⅛ pound candied Ginger
Rind of ½ Orange
½ can Pineapple Chunks
4 ounces Lemon Juice
8 ounces strong Tea
1 pint Light Rum
1 quart Bourbon Whiskey
1 quart Club Soda

Chop fine the candied pineapple, the ginger, the orange peel and the pineapple chunks. Add the other ingredients (except soda) and let stand for several hours. Pour over ice, and add soda. Garnish with mint, strawberries, and fruit slices. 35 three-ounce servings.

SCORPION PUNCH

1 can Frozen Lemon Juice (unsweetened)
1 can Frozen Orange Juice
4 ounces Sugar Syrup
6 ounces Apricot or other fruit-flavored Cordial
1 bottle white Wine
1 bottle Light Rum
Few sprigs crushed Mint

Allow fruit juices to melt; then mix all ingredients with tray of ice-cubes and let stand. When

Trim the tree with shouts of glee;
With laughter, song, and jollity!

ready to serve, pour over block of ice in punch-bowl, and garnish bowl with gardenias. Serve in small bowls, with straws — 2 or 3 people to a bowl. Equivalent of 30 three-ounce drinks.

TAHITI PUNCH

1 pint Orange Juice
8 ounces Lemon Juice
3 ounces Banana Cordial
½ cup Brown Sugar
8 ounces Jamaica Rum
1 bottle light Rum
1½ bottles white Wine

To keep this powerful punch from diluting, chill it for several hours in your refrigerator. Then pour over a large block of ice in the punchbowl, and garnish with banana and fresh fruit slices, mint, and white blossoms. 32 three-ounce servings.

Some Punch Cups

AMERICAN BEAUTY CUP

Fill each goblet to be served with crushed ice, and put into it 1 teaspoon Crème de Menthe. In a pitcher, for each goblet to be served, mix 2 ounces orange juice, 1 ounce brandy, 1 ounce dry vermouth, and ½ teaspoon sugar syrup. Pour into prepared goblets, and top with a teaspoon of red wine. Serve with short straw.

BLACKBERRY CUP

Fill each goblet to be served with crushed ice, and decorate with fruit slices, mint, and cherry. In a pitcher, for each goblet to be served, mix 1 ounce lime juice, 2 ounces blackberry cordial, 1 ounce white label rum. Mix well with ice, and strain into prepared goblets.

CHAMPAGNE SHOW CUP

Use 2-quart clear glass pitcher. Put one inch of crushed ice at the bottom, garnish with thin fruit and cucumber slices, and soak with one jigger each of brandy, chartreuse, and fruit-flavored brandy or cordial. Repeat layers until pitcher is half full. Put long bar spoon into pitcher, and add 1 bottle of chilled champagne immediately before stirring and serving.

STRAWBERRY BOWL

1 quart whole Strawberries
4 ounces Water
8 ounces Sugar
3 bottles Rhine or other white wine,
    well-iced

Put strawberries (wild ones are best) in a covered bowl with water and sugar. Let stand in refrigerator for 6 or 8 hours. When ready to serve, pour into glass serving pitcher, and add chilled wine. 32 three-ounce servings.

Four packages frozen strawberries (thawed) may be substituted for the whole strawberries, sugar, and water.